Illusions of the Heart

Mendi Hutchison

BookLeaf Publishing

India | USA | UK

Presentation by *BookLeaf Publishing*

Web: www.bookleafpub.com

E-mail: info@bookleafpub.com

ISBN: 9789357619424

First edition 2023

In remembrance of my mother Dorothy Jo Wright.
Your light will always shine bright in my heart.

PREFACE

This poetry book will take you on a journey of emotional truth and healing. In order to understand the light, one has to understand their own darkness. It can come in many forms and can trap you within the beliefs and expectations of others. Love is pure and has no boundaries, but ego built on unhealed trauma can bind you to your own emotional patterns and false illusions. Once you learn to love yourself and become more self-aware, you look through a different lens. You become one with the universe and within that, you connect to everything around you. Your presence will allow you to create a reality that aligns with your highest truth. Poetry is a beautiful form of art that can take you down a journey of insight through your own perspective and create an experience that connects you to your own truth.

Distorted Love

Seeing me through your eyes
Silent heart
The distance of time and feeling my cries
Wanting a new start

Unlocking the cage
The deception that was felt within
The disruption of plaque
Running away from sin

Seeing me through your eyes
Allowing my freedom to explode
Reaching into the cage
Feeling my own sorrow

My heart beats again
Away from this black hole
I see you now through my eyes
Just by letting go

Caged Heart

To be me again
I have to free myself from this sin
You walked up to me and showed me the way
But I just couldn't stay

Far away from home but so close to me
My heart wants to open to set me free
My mind is tough and rigid but true
Just let me see myself through you

Free my heart from this rigid cage
Let my truth walk me the right way
This sin has taken me to this dark place
But when we connect, my heart opens with grace

You come to me with this light
Shining bright in the night
Reflecting off the moon
Keeping my heart in tune

Don't go too far
I need to feel your light again
Get me out of this cage
My heart is trapped within

2

The Paper Chains

Blinded with strings of the heart
Expectations of two through paper of youth
Caged in the thoughts of a certain truth
My emotions have changed and broke through
the concrete
But the thoughts of others are on a silent repeat
The foundations were built so rigid and strong
From saying the word"I Do"holding power like a bomb
The feeling of breaking free and letting go
The rush of relief yet feeling the sorrow
It's just a paper not a cage that traps your soul
Yet it's strong as steel and takes complete control
Breaking the chains that were founded in time
Understanding the love, that we shared in our prime
With time, people can change and grow apart
Yet the memories that were shared hold a special place in
our heart

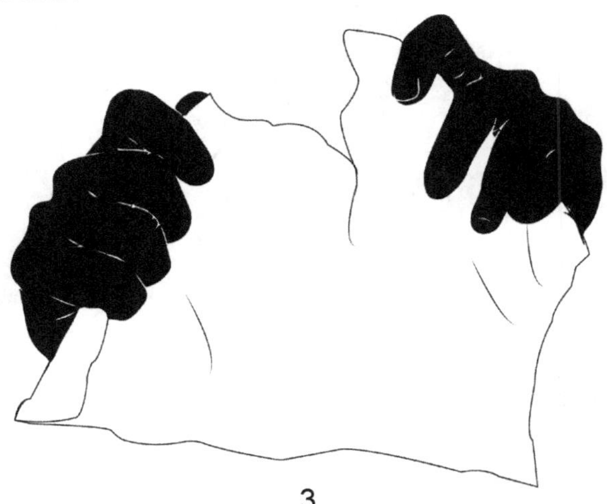

Your Heart and Mine

A piece of my heart is missing
Where joy once remained
You were my best friend
I thought nothing would change
Your heart was pure, angelic and kind
Your love will always be cherished in this heart of mine.
Goodbye Mother, I love you so
Always know, your love helped me grow

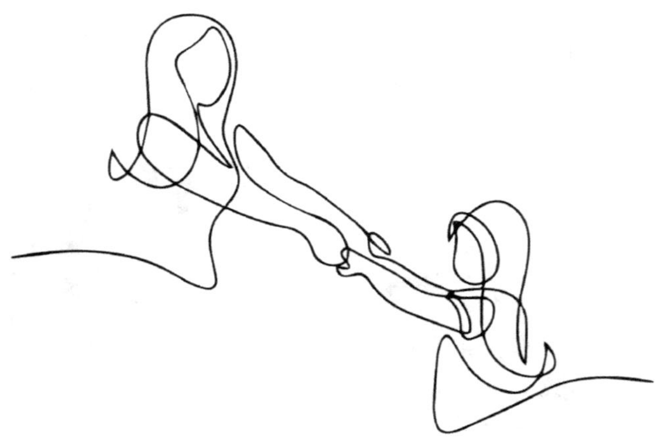

Silence

All I want is to hear your voice
But the phone is silent
The empty sounds of my heart echoes
I keep trying to feel you through memories
But instead, tears drop to the ground
I just want to feel my heart again
I want to find my way back home
I just want to hear my heartbeat
Instead of the silence that brings me to my knees
I just want to breathe again
Like a whisper of hope
I know I have to keep moving
But my heart is broken
Just give me one more day to say goodbye
To let all the tears, dry from my eyes
I keep reaching for the phone and put it back down
I pick it back up and still … no sound

The Grieving Shadow

Why can't I let you go?
My heart lives in your shadow
I want to break free
So, my heart can find peace
My Desire is strong
It beats with every sound
But I know this is wrong
My hands are both bound
Free me from my own mind
It has caged me in the dark place
My eyes are shut, and I am blind
But my heart wants to see your face
Help me grow from this and let you go
Free my heart from this shadow
Unbind the roots that hold onto the chain
So, my soul can be released from this pain

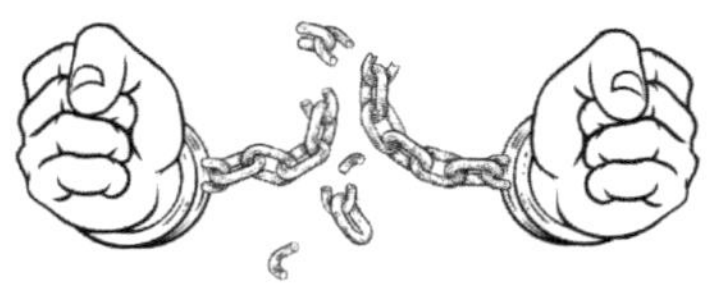

The Dark Knight

My heart still aches for you
My mind says no
I know I'm not safe
I need to let go
Finding my truth
But my ego keeps me bound
My heart is heavy
My hands tied to the ground
Free my soul
My hands to release
crawl out of this hole
I just need peace
Set me free
Allow me to breathe
Freedom at last
Surrendering to me

Youthful Passion

Taking the back roads
The night sky
Beer on one hand
Feeling high
Being young again
Country song on the tune
Excitement and passion
Summertime in June
The lake we hung out at
Staying up all night
Freedom and love
Feeling so light
My problems were small
If I could go back one night
And do it again
Sitting under moonlight

My Song

Hold onto my heart
Slipping through the strings of my guitar
Like a flattened note
Wanting a new start
Hold onto the pick
But letting go of control
Finding myself again
Through this harmonizing flow

Unspoken Truth

The sun shines on your face
Like a fire
I can see through you like a piece of lace
That burns with desire
Hold your head up and sing a song
Your beautiful voice has me singing along
Hold your head up and show me your eyes
Your beauty stands with surprise
Your pain comes with many triggers
Like bleeding through a guitar
Singing from a place that's deep
But not going too far
Light it up with your own words
Open your heart and you will grow.

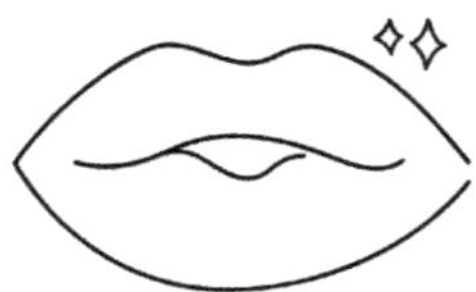

God's Heart

Coldness that blows through your hair
Hiding from yourself and showing no care
Being true to the ego that needs to be shattered
into pieces
Allowing the distractions to cause many diseases
Come to me and I will show you the light
I will show you the truth with your own insight
Believe in me for the right reasons
Let go my friend of those demons
You are beautiful, I see your truth
Embrace your light and understand your youth
Come to me and you will be free
Light up your heart and you will see

Bleeding Hands

Working as my hands bleed
Just to survive and feed
Trying to make another dollar
Just to feel a little smaller
Hope can't be lost easily
It keeps me in the game
My stress is increased secretly
Just to do it the same
My spirit is breaking
My body aching
Keep fighting strong
And hope I'm not doing it wrong
There is another way
But I have to change my thoughts
Asking to pray
But my mind is in a knot
Help me see the truth
So, I can grow stronger
I need to get away from this stress
So, I can live a day longer

Finding My Way Home

Passion but pain
Seeing the blame
Understanding the truth
But doing the same
My heart is on fire
It bleeds with desire
But I can't find my way back home
Believing in you
My heart wants to pursue
Becoming one
These moments are true
My heart is on fire
It bleeds with desire
But I can't find my way back home
Seeing myself through open eyes
Connecting roots that flow with surprise
Am I ready for this passion of mine
Pain has kept me closed and blind
My heart is on fire
It bleeds with desire
I'm finding my way back home

Surrender

I don't know what to say
I don't know the right way
I don't know how to see
I just know what's in front of me
Tears that sparkle so deep inside
Trying to let go of my own pride
Not running to far away
Just trying to stay
I don't know what to say
I don't know the right way
I don't know how to see
I just want to be me
Standing still has set me free
Just who I am to me
Letting go of what I thought was real
Has cut away all the burdens I feel
I don't know what to say
I don't know the right way
I don't know how to see
But now I can just be me

Freedom

My shadow lingers over my heart
It fights me every time I start
Free me from the voices that bind me
The heaviness that my eyes can't see
Wrap the light around me
So, my grief will allow me to breathe
Balance my truth with loyalty
Let my weakness see
I need to wash the pain away
I don't want it to stay
It broke me many times before
My shadow is to blame
Free my heart from what I can't see
So, my soul can finally be free

The Pain in Love

Love is love
No matter how it comes
It can be pure, distorted, or broken
Even rudely spoken
With the perspective you create
Depending on how it was presented
Causes pain in your heart
And the illusion is invented
Love never changes, it was always the same
If you see yourself as broken, then you figure out
who is to blame
Self-love decreases and you look through that lens
Until you see the illusion, no one will win
Self-awareness allows you to see your truth
The Shallowness, ego, and the blues
Love is love, no matter how it's given
Understand its power and be the vision
Love yourself
The power and truth
Washes away the illusion
You thought you knew
It's a freedom that only you can give you
So, allow your heart to find its truth

Your Own Light

Falling into the night
I see your heart
Beaming with light
I hear your whispers
Singing in the dark
I feel your soul
Sparkling with fire
I want to touch you
With Pure desire
The power of connection
The power of truth
Living in the darkness
To feel the light within you

Flowing River

Perspectives change as your life flows
The thoughts of your past you finally let go
New Beginnings emerge when you start to believe
The truth sits in your hands as you finally see
You feel the heaviness as it sits on your chest
You look back at your life and see the big mess
You never could see how far under the water you
sat
All you could do was grasp for a breathe
Your beliefs are like chains that held you down
Finally, released from your wrist that once kept you
bound
Your heart is lighter, and peace moves through
Your soul
Your life's different now because you allow it to
flow

The Heart Beat

The armor that covered my heart was like stone
I felt so alone
I felt lost and didn't know where to go
Everyone around me didn't know

Sadness poured into my life
I didn't feel that strong
I found something that was a surprise
But didn't know where it belonged

The emotions I kept so deep in my heart
I could express on paper of art
The words were powerful and sometimes blue
But it was my true

A poet that never expresses their truth
Is like caging a wild animal in the zoo
Emotions need to be expressed
Pain needs to be addressed

The beauty it created is now for you
Your perspective allows you to see your true
Words are powerful and can change your mind
Just by allowing you to see the way you were blind

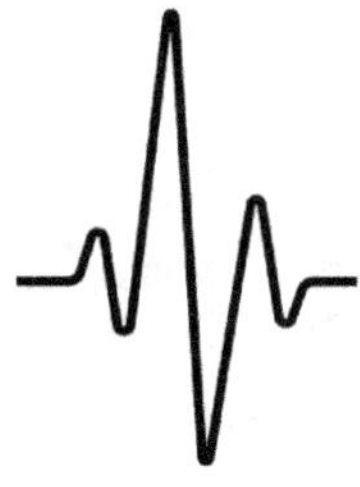

The Growing Heart

Transformation is true
If you want to pursue
It's beautiful and tough
But you learn you are enough
You change and grow
The illusions are broken
You go with the flow
Your truth is spoken
You are more at peace
As you see things as lessons
Your soul is brighter
You appreciate your blessings
Transformation is love
A fresh start
It's time to change
It's time to transform your heart

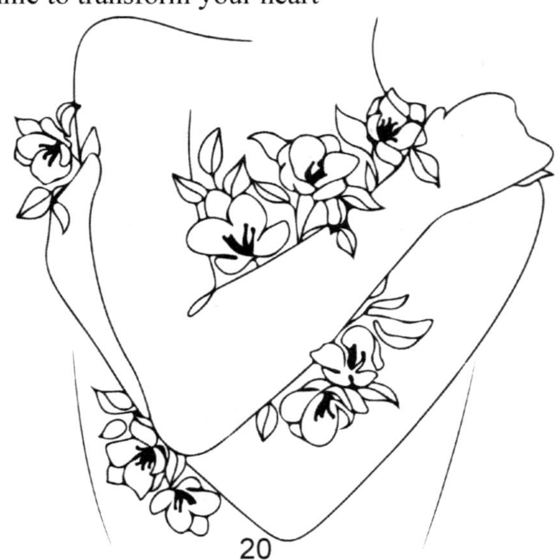

Mirror Mirror

The World we live in is surrounded by pain
No matter who attempts to protect the children
The ending is the same
The one thing that we can do to help change the times
Is to focus on our own self-love to help heal the ones that are blind
Heal ourselves and show a mirror
So, the reflection becomes stronger than the fear
It's time to be accountable and true
It's time to see the illusions that the darkness grew
It's time to change the way we think
We are all connected and in sync
Transform your heart and things will flow
You will look at life differently and your light will glow